All You Can Be

Kerry Wood
with Carrie Muskat

Illustrated by children from
the Chicago Public Schools

ARTIST: *Jesus Perez*

GRADE: *8*

TEACHER: *Jeanne Rivera*

Joseph Jungman Elementary

ARTIST: *Natalie Acevedo*   GRADE: *7*   TEACHER: *Rita Marquez*   *Madero Middle*

Introduction

When I was in high school, I dreamed of becoming a professional ballplayer. I know you have dreams, too, which is why I wrote this book.

I could not have made it to the big leagues without some great teammates, good coaches, and support from my family. I had some new teammates who helped with this project. Students from the Chicago Public Schools submitted the artwork for this book. I wish we could've included all of the art—everyone who sent a painting or a drawing is a winner to me.

When I'm done playing baseball, I will begin the next phase of my life and devote myself full time to helping kids in the Chicago area through the Wood Family Foundation. We've got big plans for that. Maybe someday, you'll play for the Cubs. Whatever you do, you will have to make decisions along the way. There will be highs and lows, and you'll have to work hard. In this book, I wanted to share some of the experiences I had growing up and hope they help you achieve your dreams so you can be *All You Can Be*.

ARTIST: *Luz Contreras* GRADE: **5** TEACHER: *Chelsea Clementz* *Columbia Explorers Academy*

Chapter 1

Aim High for Your Goals

I always liked to pitch. I played shortstop, too, but my dad, Garry, and I would go into the backyard, and I wanted to throw to him every day. We had a concrete slab for a basketball court, and I'd dig out the side of the concrete so I had a little pitching rubber there, just like the major league pitchers have. That way, I could push off and throw just like they did. I always wanted to throw to my dad. He would squat down like a catcher just like they do it in the big leagues.

Nolan Ryan was one of my favorite pitchers. I grew up in Texas, and Nolan was from Texas and he threw hard. He was known as "The Ryan Express" because he could throw a fastball around 100 miles per hour. I tried to throw the ball as hard as I could to be like Nolan. We would go to the Texas State Fair to the speed pitch machines and try to throw 100 miles per hour. My brother, Donny, and I would take turns to see who could throw the baseball the hardest.

My dad and I would sit on the back porch and listen to Rangers baseball games on the radio. We never missed one of Nolan's games. He was my hero. I tried to copy Nolan's leg kick—I tried to do it just like he did.

Nolan is baseball's all-time leader in strikeouts—he struck out 5,714 batters. He also is the all-time leader with seven no-hitters. I saw

him throw his seventh no-no on May 1, 1991, in Arlington, Texas. We got free tickets to the game from a grocery store. I was in eighth grade then. I didn't realize what was going on until about the seventh inning. At first, I was thinking about hot dogs and cotton candy and everything else. After the game, I picked up all the ticket stubs in the bleachers as souvenirs. Throwing a no-hitter is an amazing feat, and I couldn't believe people just left their tickets. I grabbed about 50 of them. I saw history that day.

I wanted to be the next Nolan Ryan. There might be some young pitchers who want to be the next Kerry Wood. It's good to want to be the best. I tried to do everything he did. But what I didn't know until later was how hard he had to work to be the best. You may have a favorite singer or a favorite actress, and want to be just like them. But you have to be true to yourself, do what you can do and not try to be anyone else.

I did meet Nolan. I didn't have time to get nervous. We just started talking. It was a little intimidating to walk up to him—"Hey, how are you? I'm Kerry Wood." As we started talking, he gave me some tips and thoughts about pitching. It was a pretty cool conversation. I've had a lot of pitching coaches, including my dad, and each one helped me. When young pitchers come up to the Cubs, I'll share the same advice I got when I was their age. I'll also tell them how hard Nolan Ryan had to work to be one of the best pitchers in baseball.

ARTIST: **Maria Diaz**   GRADE: **7**   TEACHER: **Rita Marquez**   **Madero Middle**

ARTIST: **Katherine Geonzon** GRADE: **5** TEACHER: **Cerasela Calderon/Peter Walton** *Norwood Park Elementary*

Chapter 2

Be a Good Teammate

I grew up in Irving, Texas, which is near Dallas. I started playing baseball when I was 5, which was too young to play in the summer leagues there. They would only allow kids who were 6 or 7 years old. My dad arranged for a tryout to show I could play with the older kids, and I passed. The University of Texas is known as the "Longhorns" but our nickname was the "Shorthorns." We played games at a complex called the River Bottoms and the Trinity River ran behind it. We used to fish for crawdads and stuff between games and doubleheaders.

We lived in Texas and the weather wasn't bad in the winter so we could play year-round.

Once my friends and I got the bug to play baseball, that was all we wanted to do. Our older brothers would be playing at a field and we would go to a side field and play our version, which was Wiffle ball. It's the same game as baseball but you use a plastic bat and ball. If we had sleepovers or pool parties, we'd play Wiffle ball in someone's yard. We played baseball all the time.

It was usually me, and my friends Kevin, Jeff, Billy, and Jason. We started playing together when we were 5 or 6. If we weren't playing with each other, we played against each other in the same league. We stayed

together. I was more interested in spending the summer with my buddies than anything else. When we got older and were on organized teams, we would play five, six games a week. We stayed together for 10, 12 years.

When I was on the team, it was cool to be part of a group. We sang songs between innings and when we were hitting. For me, that's what baseball was about, just being with your buddies.

That feeling carried over to the major leagues. No matter what happens on the field, good or bad, none of that matters to me. The only thing that matters is my teammates, the 24 guys in the clubhouse, who are with me every day. It's those teammates, besides my immediate family, who are the most important to me.

I've had games when I haven't done well but the team got the win. That's what matters. I know the next time, my teammates will lean on me and I'll do my best to get the job done. I remember games in Texas with my buddies and one of them wasn't doing well and I would feel bad for him. I wanted him to be a part of the fun. You did whatever you could for your teammates.

There was one time when a pitcher was warming up to go into a game but the manager changed his mind and told somebody else to get ready. The first pitcher was mad and threw his

ARTIST: **Marlene Saucedo**   GRADE: **5**   TEACHER: **Kathryn Jochaniewicz   Irma C. Ruiz Elementary**

glove and started kicking things in the bullpen. I went over to him and said, "Hey, I know you're upset right now, but your teammate is getting ready. He knows it's your inning and he sees you over here and now he's thinking you don't think he's good enough." That pitcher thanked me later. He said, "I didn't think about it that way." It's important to put personal stuff aside and be happy for your team.

Being a good teammate is No. 1 for me. When I stop playing, I want my teammates to say, "He was a good teammate first and foremost." Then, they can talk about the strikeouts or wins or whatever else I've done. The most important thing I want to get out of this game is the respect of the people I played with. You can get individual achievements but to me, the team is most important.

My dad never let me miss a practice. He said, "If you sign up for this, you're going to be at every practice and you're not going to miss games because that's not fair to your teammates." He was right. I give that message to my son, Justin, too. If you sign up for T-ball or band or the debate team, you cannot miss practice. Remember, your teammates are counting on you.

Chapter 3

Practice
Makes
Perfect!

ARTIST: **Mercy Negrete**   GRADE: **5**   TEACHER: **Daniel Gomez**   **Nathanael Greene Elementary**

Practice Makes Perfect

Today, you can learn about dinosaurs with one click on the computer, send an instant message to your friends, or make dinner in seconds in a microwave. But it takes time and a lot of practice to become good at something.

When I first started to pitch, my dad would only let me throw one kind of pitch and that was a fastball. To be successful in the big leagues as a pitcher, you have to get batters out, and if you can only throw one kind of pitch, the hitter will figure that out and most likely hit it. That's why pitchers develop different pitches. One that worked for me was a curveball. The batter sees the ball coming right at him, and then it drops down, like on an

arc, and—hopefully—into the catcher's mitt. The goal is to get the batter to swing and miss.

My dad taught me how to throw a curve. He wouldn't let me throw one when I was young because it is a difficult pitch to throw and he didn't want me to hurt my arm. I remember the first day I could throw it. We were practicing at a park near a swimming pool and I was working on the curveball. I could see the ball moving and dropping. I just started to play with it and experiment, and the next thing you know, I could throw it.

Before I got to high school, I took some pitching lessons. The instructor was a pitcher

at Texas Tech University named Mark LePori. He taught me a lot but the one thing that stands out was to do the same thing in practice that you would in a game. Don't goof around or waste time. Make sure you wear your uniform. I was 12 years old then. Ever since, I will not wear shorts and a T-shirt when I practice. If you're going to practice, practice like you're going to be in a game and wear your uniform.

Whenever I see players in the big leagues practicing and wearing shorts, I tell them to go put their pants on. Be professional. You're never going to pitch in a game in shorts and a T-shirt. You might as well make it feel as real as possible.

It would've been easy to hurry up my practices so I could go to the pool with my friends. But I always wanted to learn something. When I pitched in games, I didn't like it when I gave up runs and my team would lose. I wanted to be better. The only way to get better was to put the time in and do it right.

Anyone who has been good at something, no matter what it is, has done it for a long time and had to perfect it. And that means lots and lots of practice. I tell young pitchers now that I would work on another pitch, called a changeup, more than any other pitch. I have never been able to perfect that pitch. I have been pitching for 20 years and I still practice, trying to get better. I haven't quit working on it. Who knows? Maybe someday, I'll get it right.

ARTIST: **Javier Navarro**   GRADE: **7**   TEACHER: **Rita Marquez**   **Madero Middle**

ARTIST: *Marcos Garcia*   GRADE: 5   TEACHER: *Cerasela Calderon/Peter Walton*   *Norwood Park Elementary*

Chapter 4

Stand Tall, Even if You're Not

My dad played baseball in high school and at a community college and my older brother, Donny, played, too. I played other sports. I was kind of small in grade school but I was the quarterback on the football team. I couldn't see over my offensive linemen, so I'd just throw the ball up in the air. I played soccer, too. But I liked baseball. I remember being at the ballpark a lot when I was a kid.

Between my sophomore and junior year of high school, I grew six inches. Not only was I now taller but it helped me as a pitcher. That summer was the first time my dad was contacted by a professional baseball team's scout. My dad didn't tell me the scout was at the game until it was over. That may have been the first time I thought about becoming a big league player.

During my junior year in high school, my school, MacArthur, faced Arlington Martin, which had a star player named Ben Grieve. He was a senior. There were a lot of major league scouts at the game to see Ben. The first time I faced him, I thought I had struck him out on a 2–2 curveball. The umpire, though, called the pitch a ball. I threw another curve and Ben hit a home run off it.

Even though he had success, that was a big game for me. The scouts were there to see Ben but I did well enough to make them pay attention to me. I wasn't trying to be cocky or show off. I took it as a challenge. I wanted to show what I could do.

Scouts started coming to more of my games after that. In my senior year at high school, there were scouts every time I pitched. Major League Baseball has a draft in June when teams select college and high school players. My dad talked to the scouts leading up to the draft in June 1995. My team was in the playoffs at that time and that's all I was thinking about.

We invited some family and friends for a barbeque on Draft Day. It was a normal summer day. Then, I got a phone call and found out I was selected by the Cubs in the first round. We celebrated a little. It had just rained, so I went with about 10 or 12 of my friends and my brother's friends to the high school and we played football in the mud.

I was 17 years old and confident in what I could do. I just wanted to pitch. The next step for ball players is to play in the minor leagues. That was my college—without the schoolwork. When I'm done with baseball, I'd like to go back and finish my education. I didn't have the opportunity

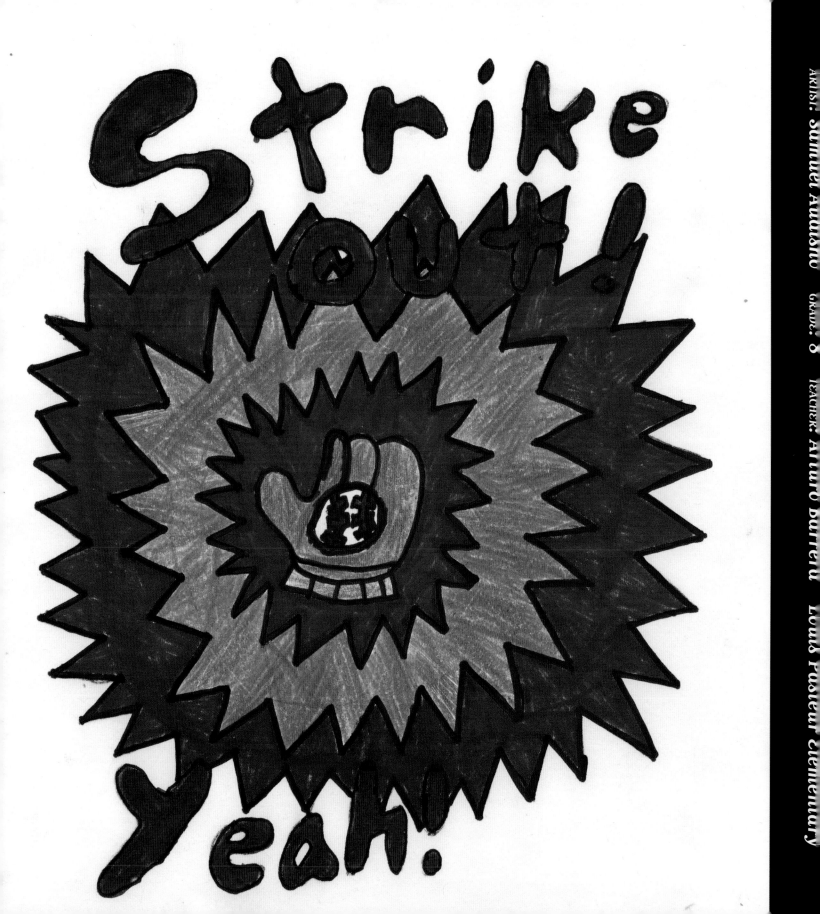

ARTIST: **Samuel Addisto**   GRADE: **8**   TEACHER: **Arturo Barrera**   **Louis Pasteur Elementary**

to do that. I went from being 17 to playing baseball for a living.

In 1998, I pitched well in spring training. A lot of people told me I was going to make it on the Cubs' team and not go to the minor leagues. When the Cubs staff called me in to tell me I would start the season in the minors, I calmly told them, "I'll see you in a couple months." I knew I needed more time. I wasn't being cocky, just confident. I made one start in the minor leagues in April and then one of the Cubs pitchers, Bob Patterson, was hurt, and I got called up to the big leagues.

My first big league game was April 12, 1998, in Montreal. My parents wanted to go but they didn't have passports, and I was worried they couldn't get there in time. Somehow, they made it. It was a perfect place for my first game because there weren't many fans there. When I faced the first Expos hitter, my knees were shaking. I was nervous. I had waited my whole life to pitch in the big leagues and then I got there and I felt like I forgot everything and was a little kid again. It was exciting.

I threw the first pitch and it was right down the middle of the plate for a strike. I have no idea how it got there. I struck out that first batter, Mark Grudzielanek. After that, everything seemed to be normal.

ARTIST: **Adriana Kula**   GRADE: **8**   TEACHER: **Arturo Barrera**   **Louis Pasteur Elementary**

ARTIST: *Delores Ivy*   GRADE: **6**   TEACHER: *Roberta Ulrich-de Oliveira*   *Spencer Elementary Technology Academy*

Chapter 5

Stay Positive

· ·

When I was young, I was a typical kid, playing every sport. I never got hurt. My first season with the Cubs, I won the National League Rookie of the Year award and we made the playoffs. The next year, when the Cubs players got together in Arizona for spring training to get ready for that coming season, I hurt my elbow in my first game.

I was only scheduled to pitch two innings in that game. I felt some pain on the second warm-up pitch of the second inning. I knew something was wrong. I finished the inning, and that night, I couldn't bend my arm.

It was devastating. I needed surgery on my elbow to repair the damage. I called my parents

to tell them the bad news and then I went to see the team doctors, and said, "What do I do now to get better?" I took one day to pout and feel sorry for myself and that was it. You may not hurt your elbow or your shoulder, but you might have another setback. You have a choice right then: You can either be negative about it or positive. If you are positive, that will help you overcome the problem.

After a player is hurt in baseball or any sport, they have to do exercises to make their arm or knee or whatever was hurt stronger. That's called "rehab," which is short for rehabilitation. After I had the surgery on my

I went from the highest of highs to the lowest of lows very fast. I won the Rookie of the Year award after my first season with the Cubs, and we made the playoffs for the first time in a long time. You think that will happen every year and then, boom, my first game in spring training and it's all taken away.

It took one year, but I did come back. I was able to pitch again and we did get to the playoffs again. But then my shoulder started to hurt. I needed to have surgery on it. That rehab was more difficult. There were days when I felt great and days when I couldn't put my seat belt on in the car. There were times when I would take a shower and couldn't wash my hair because I couldn't move my arm. That went on for 10 months. Some days, I would feel as if I was close to being ready to go, and then I would have a setback and think I'm never going to pitch again.

elbow, I knew I couldn't pitch for a long time but I wasn't going to give up. I became dedicated to do the exercises to strengthen my elbow. I wanted to get back to doing what I loved to do, and that was pitch.

I was scared. But I focused on the rehab so much that it took my fear away. I turned a negative into a positive. I learned about my body, I learned about my elbow. I had to learn all my body parts. You find out what you can and can't do. You're scared because suddenly, you can't do the things you took for granted. I had been able to throw a baseball since I was 5 years old. All of a sudden, I couldn't throw a baseball. I knew if I didn't do the work, I wouldn't be back.

But I kept going. Why? My son, Justin, was young and I wanted him to be able to remember me as a big league pitcher. I was proud of what I could do and wanted him to see it. That was my motivation. I've played five years since the shoulder problems. One of my pitching coaches, Oscar Acosta, once told me, "Adversity doesn't build character, it reveals it." That has always stuck with me and helped me. I wasn't going to give up.

ARTIST: **Daniel Ortiz** GRADE: **5** TEACHER: **Lisa Macri** **Mozart Elementary**

ARTIST: *Xitlali Sandoval*   GRADE: **5**   TEACHER: *Chelsea Clementz*   *Columbia Explorers Academy*

Chapter 6

Put Your Family First

After playing with the Cubs for 10 years, I left Chicago following the 2008 season. I pitched for the Cleveland Indians in 2009 and then was traded to the New York Yankees in 2010. Even though I played for other teams, Chicago always felt like home. When I played for the Cubs, I started a bowling tournament to raise money for a foundation. We donated money to pediatric cancer research at Children's Memorial Hospital in Chicago and to other causes.

In December 2010, a good friend of mine, Ron Santo, died. He was the radio broadcaster for the Cubs and we had become close over the years. I went to his funeral in Chicago and at that time, I didn't know where I would be pitching in 2011.

At the church, I saw all the people from the Cubs family. When you become part of a team, it's like a second family. I'm with my teammates from the middle of February until the end of September, and that's a long time. I liked playing in Chicago, I liked the people still in the Cubs family, and I wanted to come back.

I decided to put family first and re-signed with the Cubs to pitch in 2011. My wife, Sarah, and I had made Chicago our permanent home. We love Chicago, and I'll always be a Cub.

If it wasn't for Ron Santo, I might not have come back. I miss him a lot. On Opening Day, April 1, 2011, at Wrigley Field, I wore a No. 10 hat. That's the number Santo wore, and the Cubs have retired it. We had No. 10 hats in spring training, and I wanted to honor Santo one more time.

Being back in Chicago let me launch the Wood Family Foundation. We want to help children's charities in the Chicago area. We want to build a high school baseball field. We want to have school supply drives in the fall and coat drives in the winter. We are going to sponsor a playroom for the oncology floor of a new children's hospital in downtown Chicago.

I have three children—my son, Justin, and two daughters, Katie and Charlie. Baseball players travel a lot and it's a crazy lifestyle. I wanted to settle down in Chicago, because the city is special to me. That was a big reason for me to come back here.

Helping children is something we've dedicated our lives to, and I know I can do more when I'm done playing baseball. We want to make a difference with the foundation.

When I pitch at Wrigley Field, I always make sure to wave to Justin when I walk off the field.

That's why I stayed in the game. That's what it's all about. When I'm on the field, I'm competing with my teammates to win a game but I'm out there for a reason. It's still fun, but I don't forget the fact that my son was my motivation to keep playing this game.

Justin is into baseball, and he loves coming to the ballpark and seeing the players and hanging out with them. It's made all the traveling and the rehab and pain and all of that worth doing.

+ My Family = CUBS!

"Go Cubs Go, Go Cubs Go, What you Know Chicago, Cubs are going won today!"

ARTIST: Gionnie A. Hernandez   GRADE: 8   TEACHER: Kathryn Jochaniewicz   Irma C. Ruiz Elementary

ARTIST: *Shakeba Reyez*   GRADE: *7*   TEACHER: *Rita Marquez*   *Madero Middle*

Chapter 7

Keep Working—Before and After You Succeed

One of the best things about baseball is that you never know what's going to happen during each game. My fifth game pitching for the Cubs changed my life.

Before I got to the Cubs and the big leagues, I struggled. I had a problem controlling my pitches. I could throw hard, but I couldn't always throw the ball where I wanted to. My dream was to get to the major leagues but I knew I'd never make it if I couldn't throw strikes.

In the minor leagues, I had three starts when I couldn't pitch past the third inning of the game. My goal was to go nine innings. After the third game, I started to pack up

my gear. I was going home. Somebody with the Cubs came into the clubhouse and said, "What are you doing?"

"I'm getting out of here," I said.

"Are you kidding me?" he said.

I didn't want to keep embarrassing myself. But that day, I didn't leave. We talked for a long time. That was my first taste of adversity. I had never lost games, I had never walked in runs, I had never been knocked out of a game that early. I stayed. I made three more starts and did okay and then I was moved up to the next level, Triple A. The change helped.

I didn't want to quit because pitching was what I wanted to do. I knew I could do it. I was lucky because the mistakes I made were in the minor leagues. It was frustrating but I had good people around me who helped me get back on the right track, and I never looked back.

Fast forward to May 6, 1998, at Wrigley Field. The Cubs were playing the Astros. It wasn't too hot, it wasn't too cold. I was pitching that day, and when I warmed up in the bullpen, I felt awful. I couldn't throw strikes. It got to the point where I just sat down to wait for the start of the game and then I walked out to the mound.

I struck out five of the first six batters I faced, but I wasn't keeping track. Ricky Gutierrez singled to lead off the third inning. I thought it was a hit right away. It was a dumb pitch and I was mad at myself. Turns out, that was the only hit of the game. After that, I got locked in with my catcher, Sandy Martinez. That was the first time I worked with him. It felt as if there was nothing else going on—it was just Sandy and his catcher's mitt. Players talk about being locked in and getting in that zone. It was a pretty cool feeling.

In my four previous games, I had struck out a total of 25 batters. In the minor leagues, I struck out 12 in a game once. In that game in May 1998 against the Astros, I finished with 20 strikeouts,

ARTIST: **Alexis Berrios**   GRADE: **5**   TEACHER: **Daniel Gomez**   **Nathanael Greene Elementary**

which set a major league record for rookies. I gave up one hit. I pitched the entire game, the first time I had ever done that.

I wasn't counting the strikeouts. The fans were, and they cheered every one. I struck out Derek Bell to end the game, and then I pumped my fist because I didn't walk anybody. Remember how I almost walked away in the minor leagues because I couldn't control my pitches? I didn't and I kept working, and in that game against the Astros, everything clicked.

Because of the 20-strikeout game, I became an instant celebrity. People recognized me. I was doing what I wanted to do and living my dream. I made it to the big leagues. After that game, everyone expected me to do even more, and strike out 50 batters.

It was hard at a young age to not get caught up in all the attention. But I wanted to make sure I stayed in the major leagues. I just kept working hard. I wanted to pitch in professional baseball for a long time, and I have.

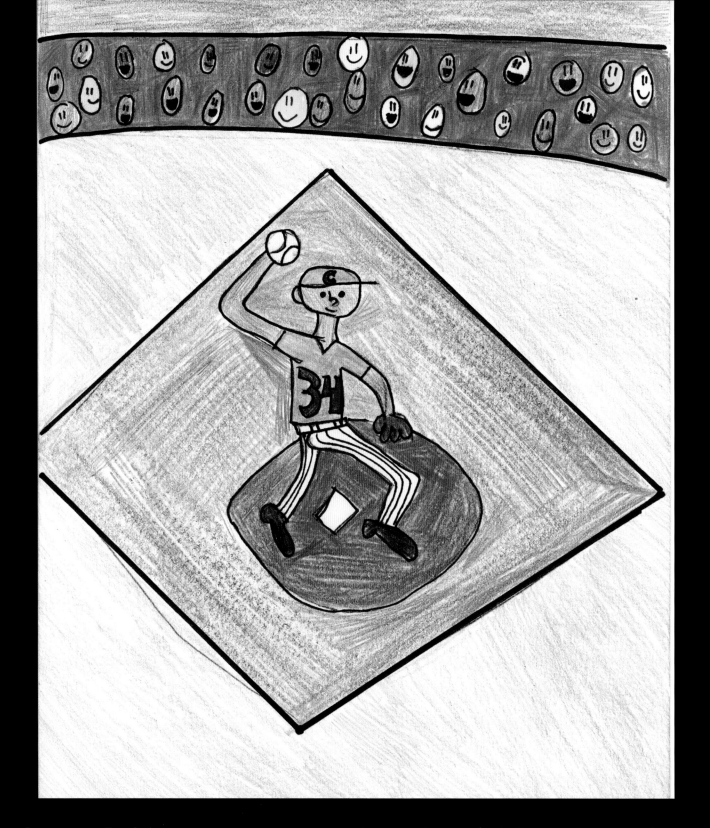

ARTIST: *Jeanette Rodriguez*   GRADE: 7   TEACHER: *Arturo Barrera*   *Louis Pasteur Elementary*

About the Wood Family Foundation

By Sarah Wood

When Kerry first started pitching for the Cubs, I was a volunteer at Children's Memorial Hospital. Kerry would visit some of the patients there and he'd play "Body Parts Bingo" with the kids and participate in events that were broadcast on the hospital's TV channel. We were able to spend time visiting the kids in the rooms and meeting some amazing children that we thought were heroes.

I'll never forget Patrick, one of the children we met at the hospital. He had neuroblastoma, which is a cancer that develops in parts of the nervous system in children. Patrick became a huge fan of Kerry's and we became a huge fan of his. Patrick lost his battle to cancer, but his spirit and the inspiration he passed to everyone he met has stayed with us ever since. He was a true hero and one of the bravest souls we have ever met. Spending time at Children's Memorial and meeting these amazing children has really changed our lives.

We want to do more. In 2011, we created the Wood Family Foundation. We waited many years to start this. We wanted to wait for the right time to dedicate the hearts of our family to something that showed how much we loved Chicago and the children that live here. Our foundation's plans include building a playroom for children treated for cancer at Children's new facility, Ann and Robert H. Lurie Children's

Hospital of Chicago. We wanted a place where kids could be kids, not be poked by doctors, or bothered with medical equipment. We wanted a safe place for them to play and forget life for awhile. We're also going to help build a high school baseball field near Wrigley Field, where kids can dream big, just like Kerry did. We also have backpack drives, along with coat and toy drives during the year for some Chicago Public Schools in need. Our foundation wants kids to only worry about being kids.

The Wood Family Foundation has the word "Family" in it for a reason. It is a family effort. We are raising our children to know how important it is to touch one person's life every day, that even the smallest giving can change lives, and that our community needs us. This is something we want our kids to be involved with. We want them to come up with fundraising activities and things that they can even do at a young age. It's never too early to make a difference, it feels good, and it helps others. At the end of summer, our two oldest children, Justin and Katie, set up a lemonade stand and they raised $68. I asked Justin what he wanted to do with the money, and he said, "I want to give it to the Wood Family Foundation." I think that's a good start.

Like us on Facebook:
www.facebook.com/WoodFamilyFoundation

Follow Kerry on Twitter: **@KerryWood**

Visit us on the web:
www.WoodFamilyFoundation.org

Wood Family Foundation
858 West Armitage, No. 290
Chicago, IL 60614

ARTIST: *Julian Gonzalez*   GRADE: **7**   TEACHER: **Arturo Barrera**   *Louis Pasteur Elementary*

ARTIST: Maria Aguilera   GRADE: 5
TEACHER: Daniel Gomez
Nathanael Greene Elementary

ARTIST: Paulina Lopez   GRADE: 4
TEACHER: Anne Koss
Manuel Perez Jr. Elementary

ARTIST: Joe Trejo   GRADE: 8
TEACHER: Chelsea Clementz
Columbia Explorers Academy

ARTIST: Rebeca Ramirez   GRADE: 5
TEACHER: Kathryn Jochaniewicz
Irma C. Ruiz Elementary

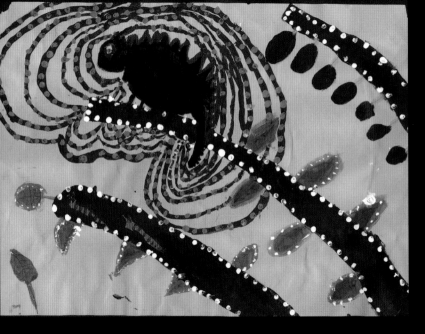

ARTIST: Amanda Alvarez   GRADE: 4
TEACHER: Anne Koss
Manuel Perez Jr. Elementary

ARTIST: Julie Diaz   GRADE: 5
TEACHER: Daniel Gomez
Nathanael Greene Elementary

ARTIST: Marcoantonio Rios   GRADE: 7
TEACHER: Chelsea Clementz
Columbia Explorers Academy

ARTIST: Angela Sanchez   GRADE: 5
TEACHER: Chelsea Clementz
Columbia Explorers Academy

ARTIST: *Lupe Torres*   GRADE: 7
TEACHER: *Rebecca Gonzalez/Kathryn Jochaniewicz*
Irma C. Ruiz Elementary

This book is available in quantity at special discounts for your group or organization.
For further information, contact:

Triumph Books LLC
542 South Dearborn Street
Suite 750
Chicago, Illinois 60605
312. 939. 3330
Fax 312. 663. 3557
www.triumphbooks.com

Printed in China
ISBN 978–1–60078–689–1

Design by Eileen Wagner Design

Illustrated by Children from the Chicago Public Schools

Family photos courtesy of the author
Photos on pages 3, 33, 34, and 36 courtesy AP Images
Photo on page 30 courtesy of Stephen Green Photography